*Now treasured by
Jean Drake — please
return.*

MORNINGS

For CC
Fondly
Eleanor G. McQuilkin

Feb. 27. 1987

MORNINGS

by Eleanor A. McQuilkin

Statue

*Chaste, as princess in a fairy tale,
but how the children stared
at the "naked lady" in our garden.*

*With time the terra-cotta flesh
weathered to a woodsy look,
an arm came off   a foot —*

*Now she sits unnoticed in the barn —
but how the sunlight seeks her out,
prisons her in morning . . .*

STEREOPTICON PRESS

Acknowledgments

Poems in this book have previously appeared in the following publications: *American Weave, Approach, Cimarron Review, DeKalb Literary Arts Journal, Rochester (N.Y.) Democrat & Chronicle, Educational Forum, Golf, The Green World, The Husk, Imprints Quarterly, Laurel Review, The Lyric, New Mexico Magazine, Poet Lore, Poetry Newsletter, Premiere, Voices, Westways, Wind, Yes.* Composer William Harper has drawn a song cycle, "Ladies of the Tapestries," from a group of these poems.

Library of Congress # 86-60966
ISBN 09608824-2-1
ISBN 09608824-3-X (paper)
Design by Dorothy James
Woodcut on page 1 by Nancy Prince Dean
Copyright 1986 by Eleanor A. McQuilkin
All Rights Reserved

First Printing, 1986
Published by STEREOPTICON PRESS, 534 Wahlmont Drive,
Webster, New York 14580

For My Husband
William Winters McQuilkin

TABLE OF CONTENTS

Ladies of the Tapestries	2
Dry Point	3
Wednesday Club	4
The Quilt	5
Lady of Chagall	6
For Nancy Newhall	7
For Helen Keller	8
Bessie at Ninety-nine	9
Fence	10
Dream of Cows	12
Forestieri	13
Winter Walk	14
School Interview	15
Summer	16
Tea Party	17
Holiday	18
Fisherman	19
The Poacher	20
Visit to the East	22
Rug Merchant	23
La Misa del Gallo	24
The High Desert	25
The Rose and the Rat	26
Persepolis	28
Tree Snail of Phaistos	29
Horses of Istanbul	30
Postscript to Travel	31
Exile	34
Rennore	35
A Mountain in My Pocket	36

TABLE OF CONTENTS (Continued)

Ceremonies	37
Night	38
Lullaby	39
Ghost	40
Rear-view Mirror	41
Dilemma	42
Low Tide	44
Momentum	45
Nonconformist	46
Visit to an Old School Friend	47
October	48
Year of Moon	49
Witch	50
Behaviour in the Rain	51
Under This Sky of Death	52
Artist	54
Vesper	55
Fletcher	56
Geese	57
The Caddy	58
Michaelmas	59
The Dying Clown	60
Funeral	61
Bobolink	62
Spring Came a Tinker	64
Duck Innocent	65
Discovering a Swan	66
The Peacock	67
The Telephone Call	68
State Hospital	69
Snow	70

LADIES OF THE TAPESTRIES

Garlanded with jewels, they stand
among the hunting dogs, the roses
luminous as summer.
They touch, they taste, the woven fruit,
explore the mandolin, the lute.
A pale stream silvers at their feet,
thin-ribboned towers rise behind them,
a smiling leopard faces front,
and sideways kneels the unicorn.

We wander in their flower-wood,
watch falcon course embroidered air.
We name the pheasant, fox, and hare,
the lordly heron, roebuck deer.
But in the hollow of the dawn,
the hollow of an older dawn,
we hear the long white gallop
of the wounded unicorn.

DRY POINT

How cool it is in the drawing-room,
high ceilinged   luminous
musical with ferns —
the portrait of a puppet gleams
obliquely
against the pale-as-marble wall.

From miniature Venetian urns
two ladies sip ice-white
martinis
at four o'clock in the afternoon,
two ladies elegant as herons
familiar with the stream.

WEDNESDAY CLUB

In the quiet room, around the fire,
you spread the vastness of Alaska, told
the solitudes, the sudden flowers,
months of darkness, trackless tundra.
I lost my way
in the vastness of Alaska — lost my way
among my friends — in that small room
around the fire, I could not tell
what hardihood was nodding there,
what piety looked out the window,
and which was wilderness
and which was shire . . .

THE QUILT

*"Work of Susie Rhodes, maiden lady -
born in Fluvanna - Died 1903
Addicted to morphine after long illness"*

A straight-eyed cat, red morning glories
butterflies
the bobbing heads of rocking horses
snow flakes, stars, red owls
a gabled house with "Susie Rhodes"
stitched on the chimney
occasional homily and jingle.
Red on white, each square demure,
prim continents.
Embroidery so fine, precise,
I taste her berries, touch her snow,
know Susie Rhodes still hides —
red bride — among the roses.

LADY OF CHAGALL

Pretending eyes
beneath the mauve and moving hair
bare sockets — lair of dreams;
the white night races up her throat
and sideways leans the moon.

The many minnow bells of town
wake up the cock, the goat,
but no dawn breathes upon her love,
only the wide-eyed dusk-blue dove.

FOR NANCY NEWHALL

*Killed by the fall of a giant spruce.
Snake River, Grand Tetons, June 1974*

My death will be ordinary,
I have lived it that way —
but you, full of strangeness,
closer to moonlight, caught
the blue tree in its fall.
Darker than wilderness, louder
than water, tangled white-water,
the wind of its fall.

Poet of granite, priestess of fern,
most inward, most raptured,
not by chance were you borne
on that ultimate river.
Long-dying we live,
roots deep in the future.

FOR HELEN KELLER

Without sight or hearing,
you still loved clothes, and jokes,
were frivolous. I see you
standing in the lobby
of The Cosmopolitan Club
wearing a chimney hat of flowers.

I see a cherry tree
deformed and dying, its blind buds
black against the sky, but blossoming —
one April limb
still wayward blossoming.
Not winter breaks the heart but spring.

BESSIE AT NINETY-NINE

I showed her the garden, the perennial border,
fraxinella, gypsophila, lythrum —
ferns, she said, do you have ferns?

I showed her the *heliotrope, heuchera, astilbe* —
ferns, she said, how I love ferns,
I am too old for flowers . . .

We walked in the woods and she turned, she turned
in a little dance of make-believe
among the moss, the ferns

FENCE

We talked across the fence,
talked over it —
a low fence, almost hidden,
rickety, but one
that had been there a long time.
Mostly we ignored it.
Occasionally you swore
at its inconsequence, I
tested its strength;
two wives dressed
in different lengths of marriage.

DREAM OF COWS

Unmistakable
even at seventy miles an hour,
the muscled smell of cow manure
invading the car —
the strong remembered scent
of barnyards
of straw and freshly shovelled dung,
of sunburnt pastures where the dry
dung lay like flattened toads
among the blueberries.

"Cows, Dad, PEE U!"
the only comment of my son
straining to catch a penny worth
of farmland, already left behind
the speeding car.
"Guernseys," I say
and hold the soft brown word
a long time on my tongue,
seeing again the eggshell light
of early morning,
tasting raw milk.

FORESTIERI

For Sylvia Davis

These woods are never quite so dark
so fragile, still
as when the cows come in,
the brassy cows with sun-white faces.
Making a pasture of holy places
they stand at ease
eschewing
the mystery of trees.

WINTER WALK

Nothing may happen on a walk,
or one dead leaf
forever fix the mind;
meet no one on a walk
or pass a bundled child
with mittens in his mouth
and be destroyed.

The day was old, no wind,
but that dead leaf
went journeying
upon the secret air,
and though I saw no roof no smoke
in all that bitter mile
the child
was "going to a friend's house"
and his voice spoke soft
as crayon, drawing doorways
on the land.

SCHOOL INTERVIEW

Matter-of-fact matter-of-fact
like an iron echo of your voice
the rails rang in our heads
as we sat unspeaking
in a Pullman drawing room on the train
going home — father, mother, son —
watching the rain,
travelling our lurching thoughts,
the station sandwiches bought
in Boston, stiff on our laps,
brown meat on bread that held the coldness
of the dark November day —

and then good God!
the sandwiches were in the air
and we were yokels at a country fair
and nobody threw the first one . . .

SUMMER

Moving as certainly as fox
or woodchuck through the uncut field,
you lead me, blindfold, stumbling,
to your secret place — a small round clearing
in the middle of the field — and there,
the tall sweet grasses blowing free
above our heads, we sat on winter stones
in the middle of a field
at the bottom of the sky.
Not grandmother and child, but two shy
creatures, locust-eyed, inquisitive,
smelling up each blade of grass,
sipping the honey-colored breeze,
watching our enemy the hawk . . .

TEA PARTY

Punctual, with pocket book,
black pumps, white gloves,
my small guests
arrived; at 4 P.M. manners
stiff as Vanderbilt
walked in the door.
Stomachs out and missing teeth,
eyes pointed in,
they stood for tea.
Conversation kept to murder.
The hour up, they didn't leave —
they lurked,
then fled, like tribesmen
bearing off a head.

HOLIDAY

Stripping
they left their bonnets, bodices,
long homespun skirts
dark as seaweed on the beach,
ran jubilant and dumpling-pale
into the unknown surf —
gasping, clasping one another,
sucked in, sucked out,
they rose and fell among the swells
unruly as anemones —
until the matron called them out
and they came silver from the sea,
the Bible class from Indiana.

FISHERMAN

With all my eyes
I watch the April stream —
the clear brown chancy water
scalloping the satin rocks,
the spring green willows
leaning over.
With childhood eyes, with granny eyes,
with poet eyes
I stand beside you on the bank,
devout as Boswell, lost
in the surface of the stream,
while you, dear Doctor, observe
the rigid trout
below.

THE POACHER

Slippering through the water weeds
he poles his skiff,
alone among the lily pads —
a banquet cloth of lily pads —
his skinny eyes grow fat
to see
such charity
in floating flowers.

All afternoon the snooping skiff
drifts drunk
among the lily pads.
A single pickerel moon will rise
before his silver fingers
free
the water lilies in them.

VISIT TO THE EAST

Like the wise traveller
who weighs his luggage
I carried my religion with me
my nationality a loose garment
around my shoulders
the heavy questions that I would ask
wrapped separately.

But it was Monday
your day of silence.
And in the dialogue of wordlessness
in the long slow moving out
of meditation, the self,
that I had not accounted for
became an unexpected burden.

RUG MERCHANT

"Beloved, the soul is the seam between ardor, prayer."   Armenian legend

Vermillion, crimson, indigo,
moon yellow —
flowers bloomed in the backyard garden,
bloomed again in the carpets, rugs,
that lay threadbare on the cellar floor.

Erect, but toothless, milky-eyed,
the fingers dry that took my hand
that took my rug to be repaired —
with care, he said, and spittle
slipped from his mouth like glitter,
with care, an oriental will last
forever . . .

LA MISA DEL GALLO
San Felipe Pueblo, N.M.

Christ is born the rooster crows,
In Bethlehem the fragrant whisper
flows from worshippers upon their knees.
The mass is over.

And from the torchlit dark
the dancers come, wearing the spruce
of everlasting life
the antlers of the deer
the feathers of the eagle.

Dominum beats the drum
Christus shake the bells.
The line of dancers moves
into the forest of the church.

Sanctus rolls the drum
Spiritus sing the bells.

Like the cadence of the wind,
the soft and serious beat
of many moccasined feet
as Indians offer reverence
for each deer killed
each eagle felled.

Dominum, Dominum departs the drum
Spiritus fade the bells.

THE HIGH DESERT

And if the ghostly yucca chuckles in its bells
and in the sun swoon violet heat, rocks
speak granite to granite with soft groan —
there is an after-scream
a fast breathing

a last anarchy in the love song of the doves.

THE ROSE AND THE RAT
A Romance

Three stones I bring you, Gabrielle,
but once
the large one was a rose
a rose carved sweet in ivory
the smaller ones, jeweled rings —
so hear me out before you doubt my fealty
for strange and wonderful these stones
and how they came.

The night was warm, the prickly sand
my travel bed.
I slept (the rose the rings laid by my hand)
I slept nor dreamed
nor heard the desert breathe,
the night white blossoms hive the bees,
the writhe of grass.

I did not hear the creature pass.

But in the dawn
my skin awoke and touched three stones,
three stones so matched to rose and ring
so cunning in similitude
I swore a conjurer had been —

but no
for in the deserts of the earth
a rodent lives, a rat which thieves
but leaves a forfeit to replace.

So prize these stones
and in the bestiary of your heart
extol a rat
which hunted in the privy night
to find a fossil for your breast
two mica stones
to dress your fingers.

PERSEPOLIS

I, too, make the journey — cross ocean, continent,
not bearing gifts, but carrying a deeper wonder.
In my silence I climb the wide and gentle steps,
steps that horse and rider could ascend, steps
that in my childhood led to morning.
The walls, the palaces, the columns crowned
with mythic beasts (the stars brought down),
are ghosts now on the high plateau, but those
who came two thousand years ago still march in stone
still mount the stairs — Persians, Medes, and following,
freemen from all lands, clasping hands, turning to speak
to one behind — Phoenicians, Scythians, Indians,
Abyssinians with curly hair — bringing tribute,
a lamb, a lion cub, wine, grain and gold.
In peace and confidence they came to celebrate
Nor-Ouz, New Year. And in the long enchantment
of this place, still come, their polished eyes
forever glancing off the sun.

"It is not my Will that the strong oppress the weak"
the words of Darius   wait.
And over conquest, pillage, time,
over ashes, earth and stone,
the wild blue flowers of Persepolis grow.

TREE SNAIL OF PHAISTOS

Who would know Greece, hold strangely this shell.
Look for the first time at citadel   cave;
with ritual eye read chariots written
in rime on the frieze, procession of idols,
blood sacrifice.

Who would know Greece, its buried cities,
see earth upon earth inscribed on this shell —
earth, color of honey sun polished to ivory,
the red-brown of earth that spade uncovers —
earth dark as cypress.

Who would know Greece, hold strangely this shell.
Inhabit the labyrinth of its armor,
take the long journey back through seasons
of evening, to the mounds of Mycenae
the stable of Crete.

HORSES OF ISTANBUL

The sun is hot in Istanbul
streets go savagely uphill
and though the drays be chock-a-block
in Istanbul the horses trot.

The cries are sad in Istanbul
the clock of drudgery stands still
but irrespective of their lot,
in Istanbul the horses trot.

For there is Arab in the blood
which stand at stud in Istanbul
and broken-winded, old, or not
In Istanbul the horses trot.

POSTSCRIPT TO TRAVEL

Where I have been, it doesn't matter —
Heaven   Hell
On my return
I cannot tell the story;
others have been there too.
Indifference wools the listener's eye
his ear grows cold.
The heavy hand of apathy
transforms my riches into rag
and I who rode the stallion home,
behold a nag.

EXILE

You talked about the fields of flax
the noon-blue flax which flowed away
so lightly
from the land.

A miracle of blue, you said
a flower tide of windy blue
more murmurous
than water.

You talked of flax in bloom
as if it were
an inland sea.
You never spoke of farming.

RENNORE

The same view of hills, horizon-humped,
the same hedgehog stone
at the bottom of the field,
a few trees that I remembered,
the trunks grown huger as the house had shrunk,
my mother's garden gone
save for one brick wall, forlorn and secret
without its face of flowers,
horses pasturing where tennis courts had been.

I told the present owner I was born,
had married, in this house.
I didn't tell her how I move from room to room
on sleepless nights,
nor that between us, as we stood
in careful conversation on the porch,
wisteria hung fragrant in the vanished air,
that from the orchard, paddock now,
the ghost of Uncle Effingham
walked corkscrewed in the moonlight.

A MOUNTAIN IN MY POCKET

Once these Ramapo Hills were mountains
austere, remote,
haughty as hundred dollar bills;
in my young sky, they were the bank.

Now I know them for what they are —
impoverished hills, small change;
small change, thank God
that I can carry in my pocket
and squander on a strange horizon.

CEREMONIES

Earlier, the ground was hard
and it took time
to dig that shallow grave.
The spade turned in my hand,
my eyes were blurred,
your childhood and its trophies
were difficult to lay.

Today you call me long distance
to tell me of your marriage.
I rejoice and send my voice
hobnobbing through the air,
but with the ground prepared
I bury you deeper
throw in the larger things
plant a tree

done
before you hang up the phone.

NIGHT

In the night they come to feed —
in the night, in the early hours
of morning, moving freely
knocking down fences
taking over the whole pasture
of my mind. Some are old-timers,
others still wet behind the ears,
all are familial, ill-favored —
but O how I pander to them!
these small hurts, grievances,
jack rabbit fears

LULLABY

"In the dark forests of Russia
where the snow lies on the ground
nine months of the year,
wolves fall upon the traveller. . . ."

Over and over I hear the singsong
of my mother's voice, feel her fingers
drumming idly on my bed,
the melancholy story always beginning
as I go to sleep.

Will another mother
someday tell of the deep stone streets
of the cities of America
where motorcycles burn the night
and hoodlum gangs attack the traveller

and will a sheltering distance
make a ballad of the savagery, a lullaby
to drowse a child to sleep

GHOST

Quiet, too quiet. Sleepless
in the stubborn night, I long
for some familiar sound
to wake the darkness.
Then suddenly
it splits my ear — cock crow
in the middle of the night.
No barnyard near, but clear
as childhood I hear
the witless hullabaloo
proclaiming
a crazy scarlet dawn.
Fervently, now,
I give it back, my own cracked
Hallelujah.

REAR-VIEW MIRROR

On this greyest Christmas day
I drive the empty road;
ahead, aside,
the ragged trees, the asphalt sky —
but miracle,
behind,
the way is streaked with gold
and jeweled children seek to pass.

DILEMMA

How to be tentative, how to be loose,
how to stand without casting a shadow

how to be transient, how to be free
from the anchorage I knew in my youth

how to embrace a palpable future
as I walk with my son on the land

I have learned to be rock. How to be sand?

LOW TIDE

I wait for the deep obscuring waters
to recede, for rocks to emerge —
New England rocks
encrusted with barnacles —
for bearded mussels trapped
in seaweed, for crab and snail
to map the hard wet sand.
I wait to walk the beach
in search of shells, sand dollars
stamped with fleur-de-lis.

I wait for low tide
for the surging of my heart to ease
for the poem to come.

MOMENTUM

I have reached a balance in my life
from which to swing. Suspended
from a tranquil bar, I pendulum
not far, for sure,
the arc is circumscribed, the ends move in,
but I can watch my shadow growing
and it takes far less to keep me going.

NONCONFORMIST

Society is a mold —
break out, fight back
I'm told, don't let
the mores get you;
so on this stage
of laissez-faire
where everyone
exposes hair
where every bell
rings show and tell,
I crawl, a mollusk
from the sea,
and scrawl my right
my bloody right
to be discreet
to have a shell.

VISIT TO AN OLD SCHOOL FRIEND
For Nancy Hamilton

Talk, like breakers, roaring talk
crashing against my shore —
towering stories rolling in,
names and places, events
beyond the reach of my horizon —
but there were keepsakes
in that surf
and in the after-hush, I found
low-sounding shells, worn stones
that nestled in my hand . . .

OCTOBER

As if fearful of being overheard,
they speak the words
beneath their breath —
housewives, farmers, businessmen,
the plumber who comes to fix a leak —
smile, look skyward,
and shy as thistledown, the words
float wordlessly away,
lost in the brilliance of the leaves,
the dreaming day

"still no frost, no frost"

YEAR OF MOON

If in this year of Moon
some of the saints are written off,
should we be grieving —
not enough is known about them,
their miracles are too uncertain. Yet
in the underground of love we keep them
and for the longest voyage of all,
when not enough is known about it
hush   hear the secret whisperings
Saint Christopher   Saint Christopher

WITCH

Not for long
not every day
not in company
but now and again
when the wind
is east, when leaves
lie back
like the ears
of a beast
when the edge
of your voice
is the cut of a whip,
then covertly
cunningly
I skip, O I skip . . .

BEHAVIOUR IN THE RAIN

You let the cold September rain
run down you
walk barefoot in the rain
on gravel
walk slowly in the rain
on cutting gravel
careless
of the early morning;
and so I fear the stranger in you
lock the door
against your knock —
there's a way of walking in the rain
a way of not.

UNDER THIS SKY OF DEATH

Under this sky of death
my life full sail
wind rising
no hands needed now
not even yours
my love
so leave me
leave me this ungrieving
sky.

ARTIST

Fritz dear, dead, I need your eye
to reconcile magenta in the border,
I need your waywardness
to let the thistle flourish
where it will.
In your wise garden, you blessed
the mustard plant, the indigo.
You knew how lilies swim
above the jimsonweed.
Fritz dear, dead, I need your ghost
to walk beside me in my garden,
to notice how the ferns do well in shade
that stunts the heliotrope,
to care for bees,
and in the dry discouragement of August
when black spot
lies, a paper mulch, to listen
to the raindrops of the thrush.

VESPER

Over my head a shuddering too soft
to bruise the evening air;
on flannel wings the great owl
swings through silent trees,
seeking a deeper solitude
within the mushroom-scented wood;
and from a further sycamore
I hear his low honed murmuring
combing
the violet dark.

FLETCHER

In Memory

If he should die before the spring
this work will not be finished;
half laid, these brick-lined paths
will seek the wilderness again,
these knee-high walls remain
to mock his scheme
and what was meant to be a garden
enclosed and chaste
will be a squatting place for crows.

If he should die before these walls
are tall enough to match the music
of his mind, these paths to trace
the litany of his dream,
all will be blasphemy, and wind.

There are no plans.
Only his wit can lay these bricks
as daringly as sunlight
only the ceremony of his hands compose
a breathing space for roses.

GEESE

In the library,
    soundproof against
        the city and the college noise,
the young priest
    was reading
        latin.
He heard it too;
    behind me, others
        listened;
and then we saw
    high
        in the milk March sky
the jagged line of geese
    moving in fathomed music
        irregularly.
The young priest
    crossed himself,
        "They've come!", he whispered,
and presently
    resumed
        his reading.

THE CADDY

Summer turns him up, deposits him
upon the golf green reaches
of the country club
as surely as the sea
leaves driftwood on the beach.
Bleached white from winter nights
of bingo, the cough still locked
between his shoulder blades,
his eyes two burnt-out buggy lights,
he stumbles down the fairways
carrying a double load of golf bags
just above the ground,
his gait between a walking
and a running pace
as if the extra motion
should help to keep his pants in place.
And on the tee, he talks —
about the war, the piece of shrapnel
in his head, the Signal Corps.
A derelict, a casualty.
"Specs" may have another name,
a life unsure within the city,
but on the green horizons of the course
he has a sinecure, a title.

MICHAELMAS

Nothing to fear, just someone walking
in the early morning
no mystery about these footprints
black upon the emerald fairway —

    walk on frost, they say,
    and footprints dark as tar
    are burnt into the grass.

Nothing to fear, no mystery —
but in the late September afternoon,
golfers still reckoning the course,
I follow with a backward eye
the charred footprints of someone
first
on the forbidden frost.

THE DYING CLOWN

Child, my son, you wear the motley
of a stranger; come closer
that I may remember you —
Toby, true, your shadow
taller than my shoulder!
A curtain hides the years, I don't
recall your growing up nor hear
your voice before it changed;
only the cardboard of my childhood
stands out plain, only the racket
of my youth is echoing.
Do not rebuke me, son,
for my forgetfulness,
the lands of love have narrowed now
like circuses, to one bright ring.

FUNERAL

Noon beats down upon the farm,
the people sit on folding chairs
or stand about upon the lawn.

I am the Resurrection and the Life.

But louder than the Word, the locusts'
song, the summer of their singing
heaven borne.

Flowers blaze along the border,
lilies, dahlias, marigolds
and the full gospel phlox.

In my Father's House are many mansions —

How cool this house of cobblestone
circled by black walnut trees
and the carillon of water.

Thy Kingdom Come —

Believers and unbelievers bow their heads
in prayer. A monarch butterfly
skips orange in the sun.

BOBOLINK

Tuxedo black, starch white,
a crisp bird flying low
above our heads, distracting us
with sharp-sweet cries

Christina Olsen buried
at the bottom of the field,
this field ascending
to the farm house on the hill,
shut now, sea-eyed

this field she crawled
her length upon
arms propped on fire weed
rough blueberry
between her legs

distinct as dream
the bobolink
telling us to leave, to leave

SPRING CAME A TINKER

Should ye care to know
how spring came by
in this Northern land
where the snow lies deep
as a widow's peak
into the summer —
it came like a tinker
bold and free
with a yellow smile
in its marigold eyes,
asking for no hospitality
but spinning a coin
from a silken purse
leaving a limerick
of lilac verse.

DUCK INNOCENT

In early spring they come, by twos and threes
up from the creek —
the emerald-headed drakes, the low-slung hens
seeking a likely place to mate —
and as we watch them walk stiff-legged
upon the unfamiliar lawn
watch them preen and agitate, delay then rush,
and squawking copulate

I am reminded of making love beside the stream,
of our embrace, precipitous, unseen
save by the picket eyes of ducks, attentive
on the water.

DISCOVERING A SWAN

Cloud white the swan
beguiles, rides queenly
on the surface of the lake
but there is thunder
in the wings
and lightning
in the neck
and cruel feet raking
the quiet water.
I fear the swan and turn away
from the forbidding lake.
And turn away from you,
for on your dreaming face
I see the deadly covenant,
in your deep eyes
the dark dominion
of the swan.

THE PEACOCK

Too showy, extravagant, for everyday —
not an endearing bird,
serving no useful purpose, ill-omened,
songless — what good is he. And yet,
turning, turning, in rigid courtship dance,
in that moment
when shiver like a sacred breeze
runs through the upraised fan — I am privy
to fire, water, turquoise air.

THE TELEPHONE CALL

From the quiet night
I watched you locked
inside your tall glass
box, the street lights
full upon you and no
sound coming out.
I watched the ceaseless
moving of your mouth,
the uncouth posturing
within that public place
the narrow tears run down
your face. I watched you
as I would watch
a bottom fish,
its moon-dark shadow
drifting in the glare
of an aquarium,
hungry in shallow water.

STATE HOSPITAL

There is a cave in whose darkness
glowworms shine their points of light
so precariously
luminous
visitors are warned to hold their breath.

There is a valley dry as death
hung with brown
appendages
visitors are told to clap their hands
and fans of butterflies spread out
palest orange   aquamarine

I go to see you, unprepared
save for the rumour of that cave
that valley.

SNOW

Still far off,
my snow is coming — hurrying the hills,
speaking to horses;
it will not fall
on the stiffened city,
but out there, in my grandmother's garden,
it will drift, it will drift.

Without ears I hear
the white spiders spinning, listen
at night
to the shifting of stones;
from a hunchback sky
my snow is coming.
pushing the violets deep in the ground.

Eleanor Atterbury McQuilkin was born in Wyckoff, New Jersey, but has lived in Rochester, New York, since 1938, when her husband joined the Bausch & Lomb Optical Company, eventually becoming President and Chief Executive Officer of the company. A graduate of the Ethel Walker School in Simsbury, Connecticut, and of Smith College, class of 1930, she later studied at Oxford University, England.

She is the mother of four sons, one of whom, Rennie McQuilkin, is the author of a book of poetry entitled **NORTH NORTHEAST**. His daughter, Eleanor Godwin McQuilkin, took the photograph which appears on the cover of this book.

The poems in **MORNINGS** were selected from nine previous volumes of poetry written by the author, with the addition of several new poems. Mrs. McQuilkin is a member and past President of the Rochester Poetry Society, and a member of Poetry Society of America.